Awkward Moments

Not Found In Your Average

Children's Bible

Volume #1

Written by **Horus Gilgamesh**
Illustrated by **Agnes Tickheathen**

About The YAMV™ Bible

People often ask which version/translation of the Bible we use when researching and illustrating Awkward Moments. My answer has been, "All of them and none of them." This tends to frustrate people right out of the gate. I presume this is because they have their own favorite version of the Bible -the one they believe to be the only true, infallible Word of God. They might be upset because our Bible doesn't match their Bible!

All Of Them: We take Biblical history and literacy pretty seriously. Before we draw a single line of a new illustration, we research just about every English language version of the scripture we can get our hands on. NIV, KJV, NLT, RSV, CEV, TNIV, WEB, NRSV, AMB, ASV, NASB, NEV, NLV, and so on and so on… Why? Depending on the passage, each translation might have all have very different interpretations of what the original authors were trying to say. Different interpretations born of men: scholars, kings, priests, and scribes - all in different times.

None Of Them: This might shock some people, but sometimes we illustrate what isn't in the Bible at all. Throughout the centuries the Bible hasn't only been changed, but added to. Sometimes we illustrate these extra "add-ons" to make the point: the Bible we know today is not the original! Some of these traditional Bible stories aren't Bible stories at all - they are artistic, accidental (or political) license, added through the ages.

Our Favorite – The YAMV: In order to bring this project to print, we had to solve a couple problems. First, we were having fits getting any sort of permission from modern publishers to use their own translations. Bible publishing is a huge business run by publishers who fervently protect their versions of God's Word. Each translation is pacakaged and promoted like any modern media, generating millions in new revenue. Second, we often find ourselves needing to summarize either very long or complex stories to fit into a very small space. Thus, paraphrasing becomes necessary. Of course, the real trick is to do so without changing the meaning of the original text.

Blasphemy? Heresy? Of course! But which Bible do you read? Who translated it? From what original text? What were the politics of the day? What were the challenges of the modern church? When was it first published? How much did it cost? Who endorses the translation today?

Our solution? Yet Another Man's Version (YAMV). Just like Eugene Petersen's poetic "The Message" (MEG) or Thomas Nelson's hip new "The Voice" (VOICE) – we paraphrase the Bible according to our interpretation of scripture and our attempt to make God's Word more accessible and understandable to today's culture. How are we really any different from American Bible Society, International Bible Society, or any of the other agencies and authors who translate their own versions of the Bible? Well – we are perfectly open and honest about the fact that we are merely humans putting their pens to paper in an attempt to try to make sense of ancient texts.

At the end of the day, we do our best to use the oldest, most authentic and original texts available. However, at times we have to use the most modern, altered translations - just to make the point that the Bible is the victim of a neverending "phone game."

Why We Care: Aside from the many translations of "adult" Bibles that often share surprisingly different interpretations of important scriptures – what really bothers us is when authors (and publishers) completely rewrite scripture for children's Bibles. In doing so, they often alter important details that young minds will absorb - ideas that were never intended (or written) by the Bible's original authors.

We encourage you to compare the passages found in this book not only with your own favorite Bible, but be sure to use some of the great online tools that are available to compare different translations. You'll likely begin to see some themes emerge from the various versions of God's Word.

WAIT! How can there be more than one version of God's Word to begin with?

Acknowledgments

Please indulge me for a moment. This project wouldn't be possible without the decades of inspiration, wisdom, and support I have received from countless individuals who are kind enough to share so much of themselves with the world. Christians and Atheists. Musicians and Scientists. Comedians and Authors. Activists and Introverts. Friends and Family. We're all in this thing together and I know I am ten times the person I deserve to be - all because of each of you!

OUR FANS - For stroking our egos and turning a pet project into something bigger than we could have imagined. **RICKY GERVAIS** - For being the hardest working guy in show business and sharing every minute of joy you experience. **RICHARD DAWKINS** - For promoting reason without an apology. **BILL MAHER** - For having the courage to say what you feel. **SETH ANDREWS** - For living it, sharing it, and owning it - whiile still being a damn nice guy. **NEIL DEGRASSE TYSON** - For your passion and excitement for discovering (and sharing) the secrets of the universe. **STEPHEN FRY** - For just being bloody brilliant at every thing you do and making me feel like an illiterate dullard. **DAVID CROSS** - For making me blow a blood vessel in my eye (from laughter). **SARAH SILVERMAN** - For your sincere empathy toward anyone suffering. I just adore you. **BART EHRMAN** - For bringing a wealth of old knowledge to a new light. **TERRY GROSS** - For asking every question I wish I could. **MORGAN FREEMAN** - For Wormholes that keep me up all night. **KURT ELLING** - For your words, for your voice, for your heart. **BRIAN REGAN** - For having the sharpest wit but the softest tongue. **SARA BAREILLES** - For your genuine smiles, giggles, and inspiring me to be Brave! **PENN JILLETTE** - For thinking before you speak - loudly. **JAD ABUMRAD & ROBERT KRULWICH** - For being so smart, engaging, challenging & kind. **DAVID MCAFEE** - For being a calm voice in a terrifying wilderness. **SETH GODIN** - For teaching me how to tell stories and not fall for others'. **FRED PHELPS** - For making me look like a saint - even on my worst day. **NT WRIGHT** - For your humble sincerity. **TREY PARKER** - For being an equal-opportunity challenger of the status quo. **SETH MACFARLANE** - For going there, regardless of the outcome. **ELLEN DEGENERES** - For standing for love and laughter. **SAM HARRIS** - For bringing important questions to light and not hiding from critics. **LOUIS C.K.** - For proving that gingers have souls. **PAT METHENY** - For humbling me so early with your gracious and giving spirit. **LEWIS BLACK** - For letting me impersonate you when I really need to get something off my chest. **DANIEL TOSH** - For being there to give me the giggles by proxy. **LAWRENCE KRAUSS** - For just being so calm, cool, and collected! **DAVID SEDARIS** - For every damn word you've ever written. **BRANDI CARLILE** - For cathartic tears, inspired smiles, and just giving all you are to the world. **ALISTAIR BEGG** - For being a breath of fresh air. **RAY KURZWEIL** - For your addiction to innovation. **CHRISTOPHER MOORE** - For Lamb. **JIMMY FALLON** - For being the best friend we wish we all had. **PAT ROBERTSON** - For showing what it looks like to make a huge profit by acting like a prophet. **TIM MINCHIN** - For ripping the envelope up, throwing it on the sidewalk, and sweeping it into the sewer. **JULIA LOUIS-DREYFUSS** - For still being my #1 giggle crush. **OLIVER SACKS** - For making the obscure and cutting edge accessible and emotional. **JOHN PIPER** - For your humble heart and your teacher's spirit. **JODIE FOSTER** - For being so darn wise and softspoken - you humble me. **DANIEL WALLACE** - For such fruitful and challenging debates without any vitriol. **LARRY DAVID** - For finishing my sentences. **KIRK CAMERON** - For dumbing it down. **JOHN MACARTHUR** - For not being Joel Osteen. **MAX LUCADO** - For helping me grieve many losses. **MARK DRISCOLL** - For not being Fred Phelps. **ROBERT PRICE** - For challenging me without having to go back to school. **STEPHEN HAWKING** - For making me feel like a lazy, whiny idiot every day. **KEN HAM** - For never backing down, regardless. **GUY HARRISON** - For giving me a lot to think about and share. **DR. DARREL RAY** - For your minister's heart and being there for the scariest part of someone's life. **MALCOM GLADWELL** - For seeing and sharing what others would miss. **BILL GATES** - For living by example, on behalf of progress. **RICHARD CARRIER** - For making people uncomfortable enough to argue. **JOHN BROCKMAN** - For helping to bring so many important ideas and voices to the masses. **SALMAN RUSHDIE** - For having bigger balls than I'll ever have. **GREG EPSTEIN** - For acting on dreams that have been haunting my soul. **JERRY DEWITT** - For a heart of gold and courage to admit mistakes. **ERIK LARSEN** - For making me wish that you had written the Bible. **DE** - For letting me stretch you. **EE** - For your outrage against injustice. **JJ** - For living out loud! **ER** - For showing me what courage and contentment looks like. **RE** - For helping me realize that it doesn't matter. **DG** - For your grace. **DZ** - For being more courageous than I'll ever be. **Mom** - For teaching me to see the beauty in all things. **Dad** - For teaching me how to think for myself. **DSW** - For jumping my bones so many years ago!

I LOVE YOU ALL!

(Except Fred Phelps, obviously.)

Foreword

Studying religions has always been a passion of mine. From a very young age, I remember being intrigued by what my friends and family believed – and why. This curiosity led to an exploration of the world's faiths and, eventually, to a bachelor's degree in Religious Studies. But throughout the course of my education in comparative religion, something became uncomfortably clear to me. While most people in America identify with the Christian religion, many of "believers" don't actually follow the most basic biblical teachings associated with their religion, let alone have any awareness of the the historical baggage that accompanies the Bible. Awkward Moments is a brilliant and creative solution to this problem.

The Bible is arguably the world's most influential compilation of ancient literature with estimated annual sales of over 25 million copies, the anchor of the powerful multi-billion dollar Christian industry in America. It has inspired kindness and cruelty, generosity and greed. It has been called on to promote peace and to declare war. But how many people truly understand the Bible's contents?

In a 2010 survey conducted by the independent Pew Forum on Religion and Public Life, 3,400 participants were asked 32 questions about the Bible, Christianity, and other world religions. The study found that only 41 percent of Christian participants could identify Job as the biblical figure known for remaining obedient to God despite extraordinary suffering. Most shocking was the revelation that 55% of Christians could not name the four Gospels - the very foundation of the Christian faith.

The Awkward Moments Children's Bible uses humor as an important educational tool, challenging believers and non-believers alike to really think about the Bible's contents and historical context. The book encourages readers to dig deeper into their Bibles while simultaneously making them wish they hadn't. AMCB shines a light on the actual words and tales from the Bible, making the some of the lesser-known passages more accessible to everyone - awkward or not!

This book takes biblical education to a new level by making the Bible truly fun and interesting. Using beautiful (though at times disturbing) illustrations, the book encourages biblical literacy by depicting scenes you might not hear in church - or in a context that you may not have thought of on your own. The result is a book that is filled with hilarious and challenging illustrations and provocative commentaries that further illustrate the many dilemmas that come along with biblical literalism.

You've probably seen a children's Bible before. But did it depict the Great Flood as a colorful adventure or a horror-filled atrocity? Did it paint an accurate picture of what it would look like if the supposedly divinely inspired works were true? While AMCB may not be meant for children, it does uncover some of the most confusing and gruesome tales from the Bible and I hope it will challenge readers to think about the Biblical "truths" from a new perspective - perhaps for the first time.

Whether you're a believer looking for a fresh insight on the Holy Scriptures, or an outside observer interested in what the Bible has to say, this book takes a fresh approach to biblical literacy and should be enjoyed equally by open-minded Christians and non-Christians alike. This book is much more than an irreverent gag gift - it tackles the age-old problem of Biblical ignorance in a surprisingly powerful way.

David G. McAfee is a journalist and author of *Mom, Dad, I'm an Atheist: The Guide to Coming Out as a Non-believer* in addition to *Disproving Christianity and other Secular Writings*. He is also a frequent contributor to American Atheist Magazine. McAfee attended University of California, Santa Barbara, and graduated with dual-degrees in English and Religious Studies, with an emphasis on Christianity and Mediterranean Religions. Learn more online: www.davidgmcafee.com www.facebook.com/AuthorDavidGMcAfee

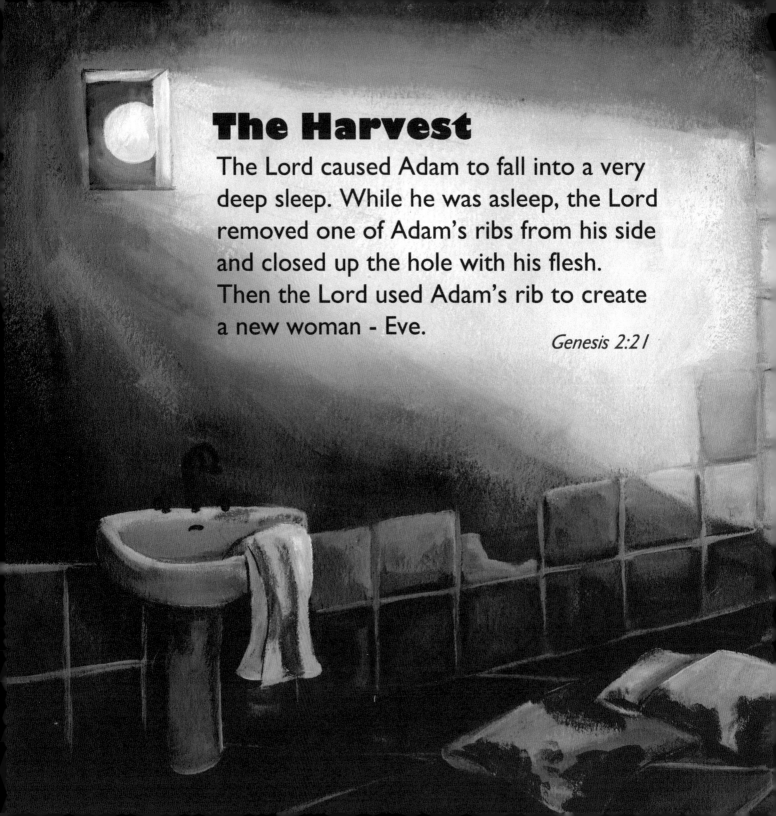

The Harvest

The Lord caused Adam to fall into a very deep sleep. While he was asleep, the Lord removed one of Adam's ribs from his side and closed up the hole with his flesh. Then the Lord used Adam's rib to create a new woman - Eve.

Genesis 2:21

~~Satan~~ Tricks Eve

The <u>snake</u> was the craftiest animal the Lord had made. The <u>snake</u> asked Eve, "Did God really tell you not to eat from this garden?" Eve told the <u>snake</u>, "Just this one tree." "What? You won't die! God just knows that when you eat from it, you will be powerful like him," scoffed the <u>snake</u>!

Genesis 3

Floaters

The Lord regretted ever creating human beings. And He was sad. So the Lord said, "I will wipe all the human race off the face of the earth! While I'm at it, I'll kill the livestock and the crawling things, too! I'll even kill all the birds in the sky. I wish I had never created **any** of them in the first place!"

Genesis 6:6-7

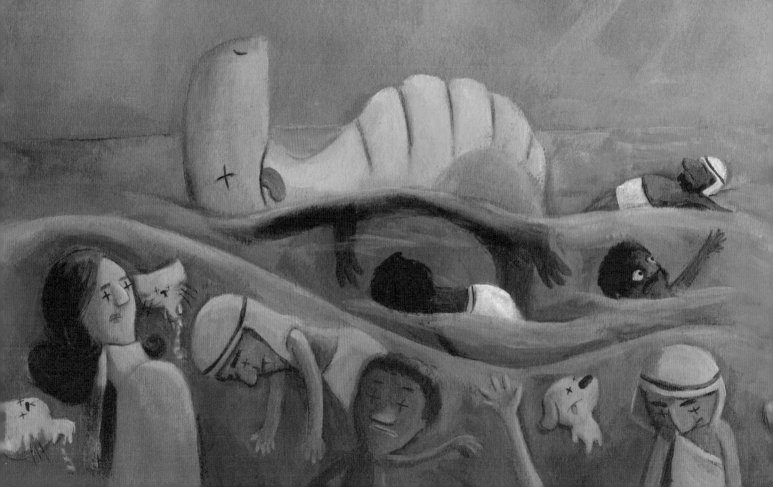

Answers In Genetics

Laban took all of Jacob's striped and spotted cows. But Jacob had a bright idea! He cut stripes and spots into the bark of trees and placed his herd in front of them while they mated. When they gave birth, the babies were striped and spotted, indeed!

Genesis 30:37-39

Wait! Not The Angels!

Two angels came to meet with Lot, the most righteous man in all of Sodom. He gave them food and shelter for the night. All the men came from the city, circling the house, yelling, "Who are these men? Bring them outside so that we may rape them!" But, Lot refused, "No! Leave these men alone! But here - take my two virgin daughters and do with them whatever you like!"

Genesis 19:1-9

Unfinished Business

Judah took Tamar as a wife for Er, his firstborn son. Before Er could get his wife pregnant, God killed him for being offensive.

So, Judah told his second son, Onan, "Go and have sex with your brother's widow - it's your job to continue the family's lineage."

Onan knew that any child wouldn't really be his own, so whenever he slept with his sister-in-law he pulled out and wasted his seed. This upset God, so He killed Onan as well.

Genesis 38:6-10

Saved By The Blood

As they camped overnight, the Lord tried to kill Moses! But Zipporah used a sharpened stone and cut off their son's foreskin and rubbed the bloody ring on Moses' feet, saying, "You are now my bridegroom." This made the Lord leave Moses alone.

Exodus 4:24-26

Get Back To Work!

If a slave owner beats a slave, male or female, with a stick so severely that the slave dies immediately - the owner should be punished. However, if the slave survives a day or two, he should get back to work! The slave is the owner's property.

Exodus 21:20-21

Behold, My Glory!

Moses said, "Lord, show me your glory!"

The Lord replied, "I will put all of my glory in front of you and I will shout my name! But, don't look at my face, or I'll have to kill you!" Then the Lord said, "When my glory passes by, I will put you behind a rock and cover you with my hand until I am ready. Then, I will remove my hand and you will see my backside! But don't ever look at my face!"

Exodus 33:18-23

Match Made In Heaven

If a man is caught in the act of raping a young woman who is not engaged, he must pay fifty pieces of silver to the girl's father. Then, the girl must marry her rapist and will never be allowed to divorce him.

Deuteronomy 22:28-29

The King Of Foreskins

For his daughter's hand in marriage, King Saul wanted no less than one hundred Philistine foreskins. David, really wanting to become a son-in-law to the powerful king, took his men and killed enough Philistines to bring back **_two hundred_** foreskins! David counted them all in front of the king. As promised, he was awarded the princess!

I Samuel 18:25-27

Tear Those Boys To Pieces

On Elisha's way to Bethel, some boys made fun of him - saying, "Go ahead, you baldhead! Go ahead, baldy!" Elisha turned around, looked at them, and issued a curse in the name of the Lord, bringing two bears out of the woods to tear forty-two of the boys to pieces. *2 Kings 2:23-24*

Consolation Prize

What you might receive for "standing faithful" after God instructs his adviser to kill your children, kill your livestock, destroy all of your possessions and torture you with painful afflictions. Your suffering - all the result of a heavenly bet.

Job (Read the __entire__ book)

Trick or Treat?

The king asked the woman, "What ails you?"
She answered, "This woman said to me, 'Give your son
so we may eat him today. Then, we can eat my son
tomorrow!' So, we did it! We boiled my son and ate him.
The next day, I said to her, 'Where is your son so that
we may eat him?' But, she had already hidden her son!!!"
(This caused the king to completely lose his ████.)

2 Kings 6:28-29+

Time For A Bath

The Lord is furious with all the nations and their armies, so He will destroy them - delivering them to slaughter! The dead will be piled on top of the mountains and the smell of death will come down from their rotting corpses as rivers of their blood flow downhill. The sword of the Lord is filled with blood! The unicorns will be slaughtered with them and the land will be soaked with their blood and fat. The day of God's vengeance!

Isaiah 34:2-8

Greatest Man Alive

John lived in the wilderness for years until he was sent to prison by Herod. When he got out, he continued baptizing people - including Jesus. He wore garments of camel hair and a leather belt, sustaining himself with locusts and honey. Jesus told his followers, *"I tell you, among those born of mothers, there is no greater man alive than John!"*

Luke 1:80, 3:19-21, 7:28
Matthew 3:4

The Law Is The Law

"*I have not come to abolish the Law or the Prophets, but to uphold them! I tell you the truth - until heaven and earth are gone, **not one word** of the Law, not even a single stroke of the pen will disappear until everything is done. He who disregards even one iota of the Law will be considered least in the kingdom of heaven.*" - Jesus   Matthew 5:17-19

Delicious Demons

An impure man saw Jesus and ran to him. Falling to his knees, he screamed, "Son of God! What do you want from me? Please, don't torture me!" Jesus said, "Come out of him, demon! What is your name?" The man replied, "My name is Legion, we are many!" So, Jesus cast the demons into a nearby herd of 2,000 pigs that rushed off a steep cliff to their death. When the local people heard about the man and the pigs, they told Jesus to leave their area immediately!

Mark 5:1-17

The One-Step™ Program

"If your right eye leads you away from the Lord, pluck it out and throw it away. And if your right hand causes you to sin, saw it off and throw it away. It's better to lose a small part of your body than to have your whole body go into hell for all eternity." - Jesus

Matthew 5:29-30

God Hates Figs!

Jesus was hungry. Seeing a fig tree on the side of the road, he approached it, hoping for a breakfast of figs. But, he found no fruit - just leaves.

Jesus said to the tree, "No more figs from you - EVER!" The tree withered into a dry stick. The disciples rubbed their eyes in disbelief, "Did Jesus really just kill that tree?"

Mark 11:12-15

Anger Management

A man suffering from leprosy came to Jesus, crawling on his hands and knees - begging, "Please, I know you have the power to heal me if you want!" This made Jesus very angry, but he touched the leper and said, "Be healed!" Then Jesus warned the man, "Don't you ever tell anyone what I just did for you!"

Mark 1:40-44

Hate Everyone!

Large crowds were traveling with Jesus and he told them, *"If anyone wants to come with me and does not hate their father and their mother, hate their wife and their children, hate their brothers and sisters - and yes, even hate their own life, such a person will **never** be a disciple of mine!"*

Luke 14:25-27

Kill Thine Enemies

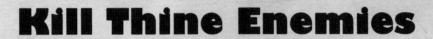

"As for my enemies, those who do not accept my reign over them... Bring them here and **slaughter them** at my feet!"

Luke 19:27

Coming Soon

Jesus said to them, "I tell you the truth. Many of you will still be alive when I return to rule my kingdom."

Luke 9:27

No, really!

Jesus said to them, "I tell you the truth. Many of you will still be alive when I return to rule my kingdom."

Luke 9:27

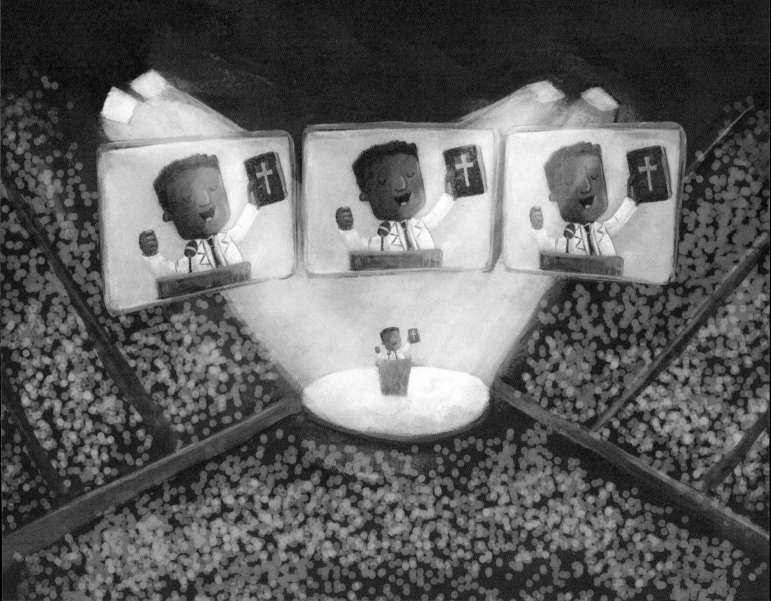

Choose Your Own Adventure!

Mark

Luke

The Walking Dead

The tombs broke open and the bodies of many godly
men and women who had died were raised from the dead
to walk among the living in the holy city!

Matthew 27:52

"Jesus is not here. He is risen - just as he said.
Come, see the place where he was lying dead!"

Matthew 28:6

Jesus Cures Cancer

A very old man was suffering from terminal brain cancer and contemplated assisted suicide. When Jesus heard the man's thoughts, he rushed to earth, pushing the doctors aside to heal the man's cancer. Seeing that the man was still quite old, Jesus also gave him back his youth - and a puppy. And cotton candy!

Horus 3:92-94

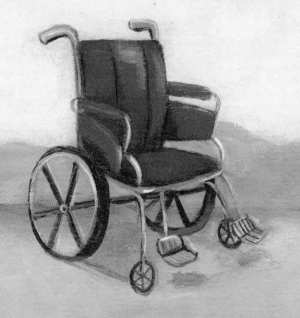

Shut Your Pretty Mouths!

"Women should remain silent at church! They are not allowed to speak. They should take a secondary and subordinate place, just as the Law says. If there is anything that a woman wants to learn, they should ask their own husbands at home, for it is disgraceful for a woman to even open her mouth in the house of the Lord - they must be quiet!"

I Corinthians 14:34-35
(see also I Timothy 2:11-12)

The inside joke that was the basis for this book.
This illustration was originally meant to be a silly inside joke. It emerged from a ridiculous coffee shop argument where a friend swore on her mother's grave that the urban legend of unsuspecting tourists waking up in hotel bathtubs with organs missing was completely true and "happened all the time." While I don't dispute the sale of organs on the black market, it was the details of her frenzied passion that led me to whip up Snopes.com on my iPhone. Somehow the conversation jumped to Adam and Eve when two people at the table (one with an M-Div, the other with a Ph.D) were convinced that men had one less rib than women. Back to my trusty iPhone for the truth.

Shortly after Agnes painted this parody as a private favor at the expense of my friend's pride, I realized how powerful the phenomena of urban legends really is in our culture - our very modern culture where information (confirmation) is readily available at the click of a button. The Bible is a collection of stories that has been passed down through centuries by oral tradition, often penned by authors who were removed by many generations from the original source. Before the first word was ever put to paper, much of the Biblical narrative had been passed through a never ending "phone game" where each new storyteller had the tricky task of interpreting a story they heard once, before presenting it in their own words to their own audience. I don't know about you, but I have trouble even telling a knock-knock joke the exact same way twice in a row! Like all storytellers, the stories tend to take on a life of their own.
www.AwkwardMomentsBible.com/TheHarvest

Who really tricked Eve in the Garden of Eden?
Let's not worry about the talking snake for a moment - it's just too obvious and some people will be quick to correct you that it was a *serpent*, not a *snake*! The real concern we have with this story is that your average children's Bibles (and most churches) have changed the characters. It's no longer just a talking snake in the Garden of Eden, it's the devil in disguise!

The Problem: The book of Genesis never actually mentions Satan in the Garden of Eden. Nope, not once! (Though, some folks will try really hard to connect the dots using an obscure verse in the book of Revelation.) In fact, in this very passage, the Bible clearly confirms that Genesis is referring to a "wild animal" that God created - not some little red guy with a pitchfork.

Why Does It Matter? There's a word for changing the Word of God to meet your own needs - HERESY! At the end of the day, yes - it's actually just a talking snake.

It also matters because there are still a number of denominations who take every word of Genesis quite literally, going as far as to justify gender inequality because it was the WOMAN (not the man) who was stupid enough to fall for this trick in the garden. It matters. It all matters.

WARNING! This is not the only Bible story that has been tinkered with through the ages...
www.AwkwardMomentsBible.com/SatanicSnake

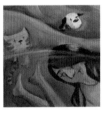

One of the best examples of patient parenting.
Most parents wouldn't think twice about reading the story of Noah's Ark to their kids at bed time. But, which version?

The cheery, colorful children's version where God chooses Noah's family to go for a boat ride and wait out a bad storm and save all of the helpless animals? Or, the story of God, our father, who after losing control of his children on earth, threw an epic temper tantrum and killed everyone and everything with a natural disaster? All of the other mommies and daddies, all of the other sissies and puppies. Dead! Forever!

As an adult, I was amazed that throughout my upbringing and personal regurgitations of this story as a happy fairy tale, I had completely missed the real point of this story: Obey God or He will destroy you and everything you love in a mighty temper tantrum! And, let's face it – even then you aren't safe unless you just happen to be related to a 600 year-old shipwright…

Noah's Ark - A fantastic bedtime story that also serves as fair warning to young and disobedient children. But, He loves you!

SPOILER ALERT: This is the same God who comes to earth in the form of his son, to be later characterized as the "Prince of Peace." Right…
www.AwkwardMomentsBible.com/Floaters

Creationism teaches kids to not think critically.
In the beginning, the earth was flat. No, the Bible doesn't say this, it was just man's original naive assumption, born not out of willful ignorance, but limited experience. Luckily societies continued to evolve - gaining knowledge, understanding, and discernment. Applying these new experiences drives us to ask bigger and bigger questions about the world we live in, each generation enjoying the discoveries of the past as we dream of the future and gain new understanding of the origins of life and our place in the universe. Progress!

Then there are the self described "literal creationists" like Ken Ham and his organizations - Answers In Genesis and the Creation Museum in Petersburg, KY. In my years of ministry, I had many opportunities to partner with AIG on various events and projects. I will admit, sitting through a number of Ham's lectures, I found myself nodding my head to many of his signature taglines based around the Bible being 100% true and inerrant. Ham's steadfast convictions do make you question your own beliefs (as well as logic and science).

Unfortunately, he is also a vocal opponent of science education in the classroom. Recently, he vigorously defended a Christian school's bizarre 4th grade science quiz in his article "Intolerant Atheists Viciously Attack Christian School" after some parents took issue with the quiz's stance on a young earth, vegetarian dinosaurs living with humans, a global flood, the "History Book Of The World," and this last question:

Q: The next time someone says that the earth is billions of years old, what can you say?
A: Were you there?

www.AwkwardMomentsBible.com/AnswersInGenetics

"But Lot was a victim! He was a righteous man with a righteous soul!" No! I have sat through too many sermons that attempt to paint Lot as a righteous man that I finally started skipping church whenever the subject was scheduled to come up.

The Accused was easily the most powerful and disturbing film of my adolescence. The atrocity captured on film haunted me, reshaping my psyche - giving me the first feelings of vengeance in my heart. I wanted someone to pay deeply for the unspeakable nightmare that was committed against Cheryl Araujo on that pinball machine in that bar in Massachusetts.

Does the seemingly glib use of this iconic symbol of gang rape from pop culture bother you? Good. It should! Does the very idea of a loving father knowingly casting his daughters to a crowd of wild men to suffer the same horrific fate as Jodie Foster's character bother you? Good. **It should!**

"He rescued righteous Lot who was tortured by the sensual conduct of lawless men. Righteous Lot, what he saw and heard while living among them, felt his righteous soul tormented day after day. The Lord knows how to rescue the godly man from temptation." 2 Peter 2:7-8

Rescue a righteous man who offers his daughters to a violent crowd (after lying about one of their virginity)? Rescue a righteous man who gets drunk and sleeps with his daughters? Righteous? No! No! No! Call it what you want, I'd choose to defend my daughters to the death. If that makes me un-righteous, so be it. This is just one of those stories that gets obfuscated for a good reason - Lot was not a victim.

www.AwkwardMomentsBible.com/NotTheAngels

I have been involved in a lot of relief work in various African countries - much of which was related to the explosive AIDS epidemic. I've been there when men have been given their death sentence, I've wiped the brow of people suffering in their final days, and I've held the hand of new widows - HIV positive themselves, as they grieve the dark future of the babies in their wombs. If you've ever wondered why so many Africans die of AIDS each year, even in monogamous long term relationships, yep - this verse has a lot to do with it. And it's not just Catholics - as many cultures are still heavily influenced by the church through the power and politics of the day!

Garlic won't protect you from the virus. Neither will the superstitious socio-cultural fear that God will kill you for having safe, responsible, protected sex with the person you love. (Sure, one-night stands happen! But why risk unwanted pregnancy or disease?)

We know for a fact that not wearing a condom can lead to contracting AIDS (which can kill you). It's a fact of science. Yet, what proof do we have that God will kill you for wearing one or "pulling out"? If you want to play the odds - be smart, be safe. But, please - don't put yourself at risk because of this passage. Don't let man's laws put you at risk because of this passage. Don't let a politician (who might be financially supported by your pastor) put your life at risk - all because Onan spilled his seed thousands of years ago.

This story continues to get even more awkward as Tamar tricks Judah into getting her pregnant.
www.AwkwardMomentsBible.com/EverySpermIsSacred

Of course - the bloody foreskin defense! Who knew that a ring of spongey flesh could ward off attempted murder? Wait a second! Why was God trying to kill Moses in the first place? In the verses directly before this story, they were carrying on a perfectly nice conversation about Moses' return to Egypt and God's instructions for speaking with Pharaoh. Just a couple of guys relaxing by the campfire, until...

Also - what do you think Moses was thinking as his wife was rubbing bloody foreskin all over him? If you aren't already completely creeped out, I should mention that a few translations actually suggest that Zipporah may have rubbed the bloody foreskin on Moses' genitals. Yep - no wonder God bailed. Wouldn't you?

Moral Of The Story - If you want to survive a street fight, all you've got to do is convince the other guy that you are even more nuts than they are! Or - let your lady go wild! A little foreskin might save your life!
www.AwkwardMomentsBible.com/SavedByTheBlood

Slavery was not invented by the Bible - just justified by it. Oppression is nothing new on this planet and isn't just an issue of black and white. It could be argued that it is a fact of nature with roots in the animal world, with a pecking order born of natural selection, the strong taking advantage of the weak.

While the Bible may not have invented slavery, it definitely did its part to package and promote the practice by providing a scriptural defense of racial, gender, and sexual inequality. That defense obfuscated the logic and rebellion behind the U.S. Civil War, women's suffrage, the civil rights movement, and - most recently - gay marriage. It is important to be honest - slavery, bigotry and oppression were not issues quarantined in the Old Testament.

"The slave will be severely punished for refusing to do his work." Luke 12:47

"Slaves, obey your owners with deep fear and respect. Serve them as you would serve Christ." Ephesians 6:5

"If your owner is a Christian, show no disrespect. Work harder to help a follower!" 1 Timothy 6:1-2

Questions: So, if we can all agree now that slavery is wrong and the Bible was wrong to have ever supported it - what else can we begin to agree on? How can so much of the black church, the very victims of the Biblical oppression in the Civil Rights movement, now be at the very forefront in the opposition of gay marriage, quoting Bible verses to make their case?
www.AwkwardMomentsBible.com/BreakIsOver

Don't look at me!
Calm down, calm down... Sometimes things just make us chuckle and are fun to illustrate. The various translations of this passage just get us giggling. (Though, it must be read with a lisp!)
www.AwkwardMomentsBible.com/GloryHole

Well, what can I say? This is one of the more disturbing passages of scripture out there. For two short verses, it says a lot...

With the first line - uh, 50 pieces of silver? That's it? What about all of this stoning and "eye for an eye" justice that the Bible is so well known for? Now to the second line - WAIT A SECOND!!! She has to marry her attacker? And the poor girl can never divorce to escape the torment of the animal that raped her?

Many might argue that this was the most merciful thing to do for the poor girl back in those days. Now no longer a virgin, she would have no real hope for the future and the rapist would be responsible for her well being - in a basement, in Cleveland, with the two other girls he got for fifty shekels.

Actually, maybe these single girls really are getting off too easily out there in the suburbs. For just a few verses earlier - if an engaged woman doesn't scream loud enough while being raped in the city, she shall be stoned to death! (Deut 22:23-24)

I'm not a rapist, but if I were, I'd definitely be a Christian rapist, because this sounds like a great deal to me! Even better - I might get into sex trafficking, because I know that I could earn a tremendous profit on my 50 pieces of silver within a couple of days with one of these sweet young things - especially for a white American virgin! *(Plus, I'd be forgiven of my sins.)*

God, Our Father. Only a loving father would sell his 8 year-old girl to a pedophile in a white van.
www.AwkwardMomentsBible.com/MatchMadeInHeaven

Seriously? More bloody foreskins? I mean, really?
The Bible is so full of foreskin that I'm surprised Zondervan hasn't released a new "Foreskin-Bound" edition of the TNIV!

In this lovely bedtime story, King Saul had a very different idea of "engagement rings" than we do today, and David proves to be a complete brown-nosing over-achiever. This is one odd act that never made it

into full-blown religious tradition and I'm glad it did NOT survive the ages. (Except, of course, for the genital mutilation of baby boys that continues to this day around the world. Actually, my favorite is the barbaric and violent forced female genital mutilation still practiced by radical Islamic sects.)

Biblical Tongue-Twister
~ Filleted Philistine Foreskins ~
(Say that 3x, fast!)

ADMISSION: We did have to shorten this one a bit in order to get it to fit the illustrated page, but you get the idea. But, don't take our word for it, this is God's Word, so - read your Bible! *(1 Sam. 18:25-27)*
www.AwkwardMomentsBible.com/KingOfForeskin

Nobody taught him the "sticks and stones" rhyme?
Try reading this one to your youngster at bed time. No, really - be sure to go into detail of how bears in the wild maul their victims.

Okay, okay - I'll admit, I've always thought of this verse in dealing with literal bears. However, many newer translations refer explicitly to "she-bears" or "mother bears" while various earlier translations do not. Did some hip Bible translator really get nervous that people might actually mistake the passage to be referring to the slang for cuddly, hairy, gay men coming out of the woods to "tear the boys to pieces"? Nervous enough that they assigned a gender to the bears?

In truth, I just thought it was a fun illustration to go with the phrase "tore the boys to pieces" (said with a lisp, of course). But really, this story is just one of the most bizarre in the Good Book. What were these boys doing? Were they stunned into a helpless buffet line by Elisha's curse? Or, were the bears actually the 1985 Chicago Bears?

Moral of the story - balding men are people too! Apparently, cranky bald people have little patience for hooligans, as well as a direct line to God's vigilante bear warriors! You had better watch what you say about Howie Mandel from now on. Though, I can't imagine a lot of angelic warrior bears hanging out around auditions for America's Got Talent. Well...
www.AwkwardMomentsBible.com/BearAttack

Job didn't just have a random string of bad luck!
There wasn't some random little red guy with a cape and pitch fork harassing Job just for the heck of it. God tortured Job as part of a bet, a wager with one of His most trusted advisers on the high court - ha-Satan, the 'adversary,' who was working completely under the Lord's direct instructions. (Our whole concept of modern "Satan" came out of much later Christian traditions...)

God and ha-Satan wanted to find out how righteous Job was. The plan? Have ha-Satan take *everything* from Job and torture him with painful boils until he snaps and curses the Lord. *(Job 1:1-12)*

The book of Job is a long book, 42 chapters long, written by two different authors in two different styles! As a result, it isn't really a big surprise that most people only know Job as the traditional patient sufferer that is portrayed in the first two chapters and the last chapter of the book. Meanwhile, the other 39 chapters tell a very different story - the story of a man who is indeed suffering, troubled, confused and terrified - going as far as to demand that God explain why he's being punished.

What does Job receive for his blind obedience? A new set of kids and some new livestock. This is like God's equivalent to a greeting card that simply reads, "Just kidding!" And that's supposed to make everything okay? "He didn't mean it, officer! I just tripped and fell down the stairs - it will never happen again!" Right...

Bubble-Burster: If God would torture Job for the fun of it, what makes you think you're safe?
www.AwkwardMomentsBible.com/JobsPrize

Where's The Baby? There is a reason that some Bible stories don't appear in your average children's Bible. Though, we don't really recommend sharing this delightful tale with junior. Before the armchair theologians scream about "context":

- Yes, this city was under siege and suffering a famine.
- Yes, people were dying left and right anyway.
- No, the Bible doesn't say whether or not the boys were already dead or how old they were.
- No, none of that matters. I could never eat my own child.

However, to me the funniest part of this story continues after this passage. The poor king had finally HAD IT! He tears his clothes, walking around the city, screaming at God - basically, "WTF?!?!" To be fair, if my people were eating their children, I'd probably lose my sh*t as well.

www.AwkwardMomentsBible.com/WheresTheBaby

Unicorns! Yes, bloody unicorns! According to the prominent creation-focused ministry Answers in Genesis, *"...the biblical unicorn was a real animal, not an imaginary creature. To think of the biblical unicorn as a fantasy animal is to demean God's Word, which is true in every detail."* - http://bit.ly/BsHMQ

"But, but - MY Bible doesn't say anything about unicorns!!!" Calm down - that's the point! Depending on which translation you read, you may (or may not) find unicorns in this story in your Bible. Your bible might say "ox." Why? Why not? This is just a silly example of how much of the Bible has been misunderstood, altered, and shaped by "scholars" throughout history.

Or, in the case of Answers In Genesis - doing anything they can to PROVE that the Bible is inerrant by cramming the unicorns back in there - after everybody else has been trying to pull them out! To many literalists, every verse, character, animal, and murder in the Bible is 100% true - the Bible says so.

While it might not seem like a big deal for scholars and scribes to fiddle with an obscure subject like unicorns in the Old Testament, what about the striking difference between Jesus' "compassion" and "anger"? Shouldn't there only be one "truth"? Who gets to decide what the Bible says? AIG? You? Me? Pat Robertson? Rick Warren?
UNDENIABLE LOGIC: God killed the unicorns. Jesus is God. Jesus is the original unicorn killer!
For those of you searching your Bibles, one translation that still includes unicorns in this story is the KJV.

www.AwkwardMomentsBible.com/Unicorns

No other name, but the name of... I'll admit - I'm a fan of *The Hunger Games* series of books and movies. However, I'm also a fan of some of the earlier, remarkably similar works like Japan's *Battle Royale*, Stephen King's *The Long Walk*, or much earlier works like Richard Connell's *Most Dangerous Game*. This isn't to imply that Suzanne Collins intentionally, knowingly copied the ideas of the other works - just that her writing may have been influenced by other pieces of popular culture that came before.

This illustration is not meant to imply that all of these other gods were the son of God, born on December 25th of a virgin, coming to earth to perform miracles before their death and resurrection. They don't all meet this criteria and anybody who tells you otherwise needs to check their tinfoil hat at the door! Using unsubstantiated generalizations to debunk other myths is a pet peeve of mine.

However, each of these gods do have something in common. They each contain various attributes and themes coming from their predecessors. To be fair, this problem of coincidental similarities with previous deities is not unique to Christianity.

My point? If the Wachowski Brothers had written The Matrix two thousand years ago, at a time when it wasn't as easy to research, cross-reference, debate, and de-bunk claims of authors and orators - would we be praying to Neo today? If Harry Potter were written in the time of Moses, would we deny all personal responsibility for our actions by blaming all of the evil in the world on Lord Voldemort?

It is easy to dismiss the idea of Neo or Voldemort as pure fiction - based on the myths, traditions and fantasies of our time. But what about all of the other gods that came before Jesus? What about Jesus?!

www.AwkwardMomentsBible.com/NoOtherName

Didn't anybody bother to issue an Amber Alert?
Confession: I am a history whore. I spend most of my

(limited) reading time these days with my nose in books covering interesting events of world history or the biographies of the heroes, leaders, and villains of our past. I love the level of detail!

By the time I was 13 I had my first job. At 16, I lost my virginity. At 17, I dropped out of high school to start a business and go to college early. When I was 19, I witnessed my first horrific death. By 20, I had sold my business and converted from Catholicism to begin exploring the Protestant world. By the time I was 22 I was married with two kids and working in full time ministry. At 28 I had the first major accident in my life. By 29, I was divorced. By the time I was 30, I was remarried and pursuing a completely different career that eventually led me to where I sit today. My point? Who cares, I'm a complete nobody! Yet many of the most important, impactful, and influential experiences in my life took place in my teens and twenties.

I guess my question is: If you were writing the biography of Jesus Christ, the Messiah, the savior of the world - wouldn't you think it was a good idea to include a little backstory? I don't need to know what he ate for breakfast, but what was he up to for these 18 years? *(30, if you miss Luke 2:41-52.)*

Was he educated or a dropout? Was he an introverted hermit? Was he already healing the sick? Or was he an outlaw in jail for robbery and the attempted murder one of his teachers? When did this little boy become the Jesus we hear about in church? Sure, the writers of the Gospels may not have been with Jesus during this time. But here's a news flash: they weren't hanging out with Jesus later on, either...

www.AwkwardMomentsBible.com/TheRunaway

Truly, the greatest man to walk the earth.
Most folks these days might not take kindly to their prophet hanging out with a homeless ex-con living under a bridge down by the river, living off bugs.

The Gospel of Luke starts with the the foretelling of the birth (and life) of John the Baptist before moving on to the birth of Jesus in Luke 2. John was definitely an interesting figure who had one of the most interesting deaths in the entire Bible, but we'll save that for the next book.

What some people miss is that the last time we heard from Jesus was at the end of Luke 2, when he is referenced (briefly) as a twelve-year-old. Fast forward eighteen years, where the story picks back up with John getting out of prison, when he meets Jesus and baptizes him among others followers. John, the homeless ex-con hermit in the woods, living off bugs and honey, swimming in the river with friends every day? Yep - I guess I can see Jesus' point - John had it all! This is how I spent my summers in college!

WARNING: This is a satirical point of view, a parody, comedy. It is not meant to ruin your day or kick your metaphorical puppy. It is meant to encourage people to think about stories and contexts outside of the traditional narrative they may have settled on (and forgotten about) decades earlier.

www.AwkwardMomentsBible.com/GreatestMan

"But, the Old Testament is ancient and doesn't matter any more! Jesus changed everything - you need to understand HIS words!"

We have all heard the contradictory cherry picking. Slavery is suddenly wrong, but gays are an abomination. You can eat shrimp, but rapists might actually go to jail today. Alright, well - here are Jesus' own words again to clear up the confusion. This time from Luke 16:17...

"The law hasn't lost its force. It is easier for heaven and earth to disappear than for the smallest dot of God's law to be dropped." - Jesus

He seems to speak pretty clearly about the Law. It wasn't until the last 50 years that theologians have scrambled to distance Christianity from other barbaric religious practices that this notion of the Old Testament being "irrelevant" began to spring up. Some theologians will even stretch to say that Jesus was speaking in some sort of cryptic code, claiming that what He was really saying was that the Law only mattered until his death and resurrection. Well, then what? The Law doesn't matter anymore? Which parts?

I'm sorry, but this seems like far too convenient a case of revisionist history in a blatant attempt to blur the lines over the Bible's negative influences in modern culture - slavery, homophobia, gender inequality, child abuse, and on and on... You can't say that the Old Testament doesn't matter one moment, but then use it to justify hate and influence elections the next.

Think! Without the Old Testament, there would be no creation, no Original Sin, no institution of marriage, no Noah's ark, no promise of The Redeemer, no Ten Commandments, no crossing of the Red Sea - and, most importantly - there would be no prophecy of a coming Messiah to later be filled by Jesus. That's right - without the Old Testament, there would be no New Testament!

Here is another another Awkward Moment straight from the mouth of Jesus, where he reminds his followers of the importance of the Law.

"For God said, 'Respect your father and your mother,' and 'If you curse your father or your mother, you are to be put to death.' But some of you reject this Law. You now say that if people have something they could use to help their father or mother, but say, 'This belongs to God,' they do not need to honor their father. In this way you disregard God's command, in order to follow your own teaching. You hypocrites!" Matt 15:4-7

That's right, folks - Jesus was pretty clear. If you ignore God's Law in favor of man's easier law, Jesus considers you a hypocrite! (And, we all know what happens to hypocrites in the Bible...)

The Point? If you want to believe the Bible is the Word of God and follow it word for word - well, then you have to believe the WHOLE BIBLE - not just the parts that you like. Be careful what you wish for and be prepared to pay the price.

Illustrated References:
"Raped In The City" (Deut 22:27)
"Worked on The Sabbath" (Exodus 31:14)
"Yelled At Mommy" (Exodus 21:17)
"Made A Potion" (Exodus 22:18)
"Raped By Farmer" (Lev 20:16)
"Lied About Virginity" (Deut 22:20-12)
"Told Joke About God" (Lev 24:14-16, 23)

www.AwkwardMomentsBible.com/NotOneWord

Demonic Bacon? No commentary necessary, really... Agnes just wanted to illustrate mass pig suicides for some reason. FREE ADVICE: You might not want to read this to your kids after watching *Babe*.

www.AwkwardMomentsBible.com/DemonicBacon

What happens when your right eye offends God?

Pluck it out! What happens when your left eye offends God? Keep plucking! This verse brings new meaning to the phrase "Blind Obedience."

Throughout history, there has never been a more effective recovery program for any addiction. Say the Lord's name in vain - tear your tongue out! Paint an illustration of the original Greek translation of Jesus and the leper - saw your hand off! Listen to a scholarly lecture on the Johannine Comma - slice your ear off! Have a nocturnal emission? Bad news...

Has all of this self-mutilation actually brought you any closer to God? Have you lost all the limbs necessary to give yourself fully to the Lord, regardless of your own instincts, experiences and perceptions? Or, are you able to still THINK for yourself? If so, it's time for your scheduled frontal lobotomy.

www.AwkwardMomentsBible.com/PluckItOut

The Westboro Baptist Church *klan* has it wrong!

It's FIGS that God hates – not (the hate-filled slang term for homosexuals). Actually, Jesus was apparently a huge fan of figs. So much so that he got angry with a fig tree that wouldn't make fruit. So, he killed it! Naturally. I mean, who wouldn't? It couldn't have just been the wrong season, right?

Wait just a minute! Why didn't Jesus just perform a miracle for the tree to produce fruit instead? By killing the tree he still goes away hungry. What would Jesus eat? (WWJE™) What did his disciples learn that day?

I'll admit – as much as I can't stand Fred Phelps or what his "people" stand for, a Christian friend recently made a great point: It's people like Phelps who remind us all (Atheists, Christians, Muslims, Democrats, Bieber-Fans) how fine the line is between having convictions and being bat-sh*t crazy! And for that, Freddy– we thank you!

www.AwkwardMomentsBible.com/GodHatesFigs

*"Your a stupid f***ing liar! Why would Jesus get angry at a lepper! The Bible dont say this! It says Jesus did pity! You should ashamed of yourself a**hole!"* - #1 Fan [sic, sic, sic, sic]

I am always amazed by how many people completely ignore the footnotes of their Bibles. Then I remember the studies showing how often people actually read their Bibles, and to what extent. I have at least ten different print translations right here on my shelf that all concede the original Greek was "orgistheis" - a word with really only one translation - anger. However, this original context is always hidden as part of the footnotes. The footnotes! This begs the question: Why are publishers purposefully hiding the most original, most accurate translation on ANY scripture in the footnotes?

If you are confused why so many Bibles use the wrong (new/changed) translation of this verse, rather than the oldest, most original Greek - ask you pastor about the Greek words *orgistheis, embrimesamenos,* and *exebalen.* Then, think about it on your own and maybe do a little research on other important verses in the Bible that have been altered through the ages.

www.AwkwardMomentsBible.com/AngerManagement

"Jesus didn't really mean to hate everyone! You need to study more to understand what he meant!"

The original Greek word "miseo" used here in Luke has a pretty specific meaning: hate. In fact, it's an even stronger word than we have today - Jesus used it in Matthew 5:21–23 to warn people that anger (expressed with this 'miseo') against someone is tantamount to murder! **Murder!**

To defend this verse by saying, "Jesus didn't mean 'hate'" is reaching a little too far to try and explain what Jesus "really" meant. In fact, I have sat through many Bible studies and read many long explanations of this passage. Every author/leader has one thing in common: they have their own "spin" to try and justify how and why Jesus didn't mean what he said. I'm no expert, but - isn't that heresy?

"Just as damaging as a madman shooting a deadly weapon - is someone who lies to a friend and then says, 'I was just kidding.'" - Proverbs 26:18-19

Over the centuries Luke 14 has been slowly modified to be more acceptable to most readers. Some modern translations have even gone as far as to remove the word "hate" altogether and rephrase the verse along the lines, "If you don't love me even more than you already love your father..." Heresy!

The Gospel of Matthew has a very similar passage, but being based on the earlier work of Luke was already starting to sport a tamer version that was easier to understand and accept in a likely attempt to portray a Jesus that was a bit more palatable to the masses. Just think - the earliest "tweaks" to the original story started almost 2,000 years ago! Now think of the effect of playing the "telephone game" for twenty centuries...

So, the takeaway is that "we are supposed to hate our own lives because we are worthless without Jesus." This is how a good friend (and theologian with a Ph.D. in Biblical History) explained it to me with a straight face. As if serving a megalomaniacal God who looks down on us as 'worthless' is a good thing?

John even uses the same word to make his point in 1 John 3:15, *"Everyone who hates his brother is a murderer."* That's right, in order to follow Christ, you must be willing to be a murderer!

www.AwkwardMomentsBible.com/HateEveryone

CALM DOWN! This is an illustration of context. Many would claim that this verse is taken out of context, which - I fully admit is true. Well, partially. You see, Jesus never said these words himself. Except, well - he did. (Are you confused yet?) Jesus told his disciples a lot of stories - choosing his words wisely, with purpose and timing - never by accident. Jesus also made no apologies for the need to uphold his Father's Law.

The verse is taken from the last line of a parable where an unpopular king left town for a while, after first giving each of his servants some money (ten minas). When the king got back, he asked each servant what they did with the money. Those who invested it and made more money for the king were rewarded. One servant was afraid of losing his master's money so he hid it for safekeeping. As a result, he was punished. Severely. Jesus ends the story powerfully with the verses quoted in the illustration - presenting the actions of an unpredictable king.

Why was Jesus telling this story? To give a lecture on financial investments? (Maybe.) To ridicule the king for his vengeance? (He doesn't.) Or, to warn of what happens to those who do not follow their king? To understand the **context**, Jesus is telling this story to his followers as they sit outside of Jerusalem, fully expecting that the Kingdom of God will appear "immediately" with Jesus as *their* king on the throne.

Why have so many translations of this last verse been altered through the ages from "slaughter," "kill," or "slay" to "remove them from my sight"? Yet, confusing passages remain where Jesus kills harmless trees or advocates the stoning of disobedient children. Why then, is it really so unthinkable that Jesus might exhibit some of the same vengeful tendencies as his own Father (Himself)? How many times had God (who, remember, came to earth in the form of the Son) already slaughtered the masses? The same God who sent the mighty flood, sent the plagues, killed all of the firstborns of Egypt, or, just tortured Job for the fun of it. Suddenly this same God wouldn't demand the killing of His enemies? Why not? Why the sudden personality shift from His demonstrably consistent history of smiting at will? To ancient readers of the Infancy Gospel of Thomas, this Jesus would have been no surprise. After all, He certainly already had plenty of practice killing His enemies without apology. God slaughtered innocent babies and helpless unicorns. Jesus is God. Therefore... (We'll let you discover the next logical conclusion of basic transitive properties of the Trinity on your own.)

I fully admit - there is a lot of "context" to understand with this passage! Another bit of context that many Christians might be unaware of is that Jesus is actually a central figure to Islam - the Masih (Messiah), a respected and revered prophet. So important, in fact, that he is mentioned twenty-five times in the Qur'an where Muhammad is only mentioned five times by name. How dare we conveniently condemn the violent actions of a few radical muslims while ignoring the countless slaughters at the hands of the Christian God and His followers! The Flood, the plagues, the Crusades, the Holocaust, the KKK, bombed abortion clinics, hate crimes against gays, domestic abuse, wars against non-Christian nations?

www.AwkwardMomentsBible.com/JihadJesus

"Jesus is returning soon! He is coming back for me!"
I will admit, this idea kept me out of a lot of trouble through my formative years into adulthood. Jesus could be here any day! The mere thought of getting caught with my pants down had me living on the straight and narrow.

It wasn't really until I was in the process of leaving the ministry that it dawned on me - I wasn't the only person in history to have felt this way - to *know* it was true. In fact, there were billions before me who had lived in their own "end times" - sharing the same overwhelming certainty, now in their graves. Starting with Jesus' disciples, every generation had one thing in common: they were *wrong* about the Rapture.

www.AwkwardMomentsBible.com/ComingSoon

Can vegetarians and vegans take communion?
"Drink his blood? That's disgusting!!" daughter, 9
"Eat him? Which parts?" son, 7

Growing up in the Catholic church and spending the majority of my adult life involved in ministry, it wasn't until I had to explain the act of Communion to my own children that I was forced to take a step back and really think about what it looked like to "outsiders" who had never taken their first gulp.

My kids' questions might seem childlike and naive. But, I had to ask myself, "Wait, wait - if I hadn't been raised in the church, drinking the Kool-Aid and eating Saltines since before I could ride a bike, what would I think of this act?" And I hadn't even explained the concept of transubstantiation to them yet!

Many would claim (these days) that the whole idea of communion is meant to be symbolic, without any roots in pagan blood rituals. Yet Jesus' words are pretty darn explicit, repetitive, and clear to me. *Real* food, *real* drink. Symbolic or otherwise, it is a difficult passage to swallow. Literally.

www.AwkwardMomentsBible.com/LastSupper

What did the Bible say about Jesus? It depends.

Most readers combine, mix and match different verses from different gospels (which were written by different authors at different times for different audiences) to come up with their own Super Gospel - a completely new account of events that defy all laws of logic, time, and space. This is called HARMONIZATION - a fancy word for blasphemy.

Each author of the Gospels was writing *their* own Gospel - *their* accounts of the life and times of Jesus, through *their* eyes, intended for *their* audiences. Of course they'll all see things a little differently, just like eyewitnesses to a crime - everybody has their own view of what happened. So, who is right? What is ***the*** truth?

To be clear - the Bible is full of thousands of contradictions and discrepancies - some are tiny; some are enormous. In "The Passion" narratives, Matthew, Mark, Luke and John all have very different accounts of the last hours of Jesus' life and his resurrection from the grave. To be clear - we aren't talking about the little differences - we are talking about differences that have baffled scholars and theologians for centuries!

Who was Jesus? Was he crying out in confused agony, angry with God? Was he calm and consoling, reassuring his followers that this was all planned and that he was at peace? Much like a crime scene, regardless of how many witnesses there are, there can only be ***one*** truth.

To me, these are some of the most important foundational questions we must ask of the Bible.

FUN GAME: Please remember - according to the doctrine of the trinity, Jesus was God Himself, in the flesh. Now, go back and re-read some of the Old Testament and imagine Jesus carrying out various acts that we usually attribute to some cranky "old" God. Don't blame me - the Bible tells us they are one and the same!

The God of the Old Testament is the Jesus of the New Testament and can not be ignored.

www.AwkwardMomentsBible.com/Harmonized

If you've been to church on Easter in the last fifty years, you've probably heard the pastor call out, *"He Is Risen,"* with the congregation trained and expected to answer, *"He Is Risen, Indeed!"*

I've always been a little uncomfortable with chanting anything in a monotone voice, as it reminds me of zombies walking the streets with their eyes rolled back in their heads. This got me thinking about the saints that rose from their tombs when Jesus died on the cross. From there, it was a short hop to think about Jesus rising from the dead to walk among the living. The walking dead.

This illustration is dealing with two separate (but related) sections of scripture to illustrate the point.

He Is Risen!
(Run for your lives....)
He Is Risen Indeed!"

Sorry folks, a zombie is a zombie...

www.AwkwardMomentsBible.com/HeIsRisen

What, you haven't seen this verse? No surprise...

There are many lesser-known Gospels that didn't make the final cut when the powerful decision makers of their day assembled what we now refer to as the New Testament.

Contrary to popular belief, a high priest did not just find the New Testament sitting on his doorstep one morning. It was written by man and assembled by man, the result of a great deal of politics, editing, marketing, negotiating, and - more editing. Much discussion (and fighting) went into deciding which Gospels made it into the Good Book, while others were thrown out as heresy. The Proto-Gospel of James, History of Joseph, The Carpenter, the Infancy Gospel of Thomas, and - my favorite, The Greater Questions Of Mary. These writings all painted a picture of what the earliest Christians "knew" of Jesus at the time.

The big question I have is - who got to decide what was "fact" and what was "fiction" back in the day? In modern terms, who be the trusted decision makers of today? A "prophet" like Pat Robertson? A fundamentalist like Fred Phelps? A celebrity like Joel Osteen or Jesus Daily? Most of these decisions were being made 100-300 years after the books were written (which were often written a full generation after the events took place). Hundreds of years, hundreds of stories and storytellers.

Of course, this passage isn't part of the Bible. I made it up to serve my own purposes. Just as the leaders of the day coerced Erasmus to add the Johannine Comma, the only explicit mention of the Trinity to 1 John 5:7–8 way back in 1552 (*a long time after the New Testament was written*).

www.AwkwardMomentsBible.com/LostPassage

Well, what can you say? No, really - this question is for the ladies: What can YOU say? Not much, apparently. In an article titled "May Women Speak In Church," author James Scott puts his own spin on this troubling bit of scripture (that simply reiterates a Biblical theme about how wicked, stupid, and worthless women are).

"The Bible teaches that women are not to speak in church. The fact that our society is in rebellion against the biblical teaching regarding women does not make the

Bible obsolete; it makes us who adopt the world's values shameful and dishonoring to the Lord." - James W. Scott, New Horizons www.opc.org/new_horizons/9601a.html

Who can argue with Mr. Scott's analysis? It is THE Bible. This article reminded me of more passages that remind us it was the woman (Eve) who was stupid enough to fall for the old "talking-snake-forbidden-fruit" trick. A man would never be that dumb, right? However, I suppose a neverending "time-out" as punishment for being a victim of blatant entrapment isn't the worst sentence for destroying man's chance of eternal happiness by eating an apple.

The message to women is clear: You are welcome to come to church, but please keep your pretty mouths shut! (Also, enjoy your fight for the right to vote and ability to earn an equal wage.)

www.AwkwardMomentsBible.com/Silence

The Endless Loop

You Will Burn In Hell For Eternity! (Unless...)

ALRIGHT, YOU GOT ME... UNLESS WHAT?

UNLESS YOU ACCEPT JESUS AS YOUR LORD AND PERSONAL SAVIOR!

BUT, WHY WOULD I DO THAT?

BECAUSE THE BIBLE TELLS US TO!

BUT, HOW CAN I TRUST THE BIBLE?

BECAUSE THE BIBLE IS THE INFALLIBLE WORD OF GOD!

ACCORDING TO ???

THE BIBLE!!!

BUT, WHAT IF I DON'T TRUST THE BIBLE?

You Will Burn In Hell For Eternity! (Unless...)

READ MY SIGN!!!

UNLESS WHAT, AGAIN?

TO BE CONTINUED...
(for generations)

This is how I spend most of my mornings these days - answering email. This was inspired by many real-life experiences throughout my years on BOTH sides of this argument. Yes, I've even uttered the phrase, "Because the Bible tells me so!" No, I've never carried a sign.

How do we have more open and intelligent conversations about the Bible, without getting stuck in a maze of circular logic? I'm not sure what else to say, so I'll just let the comic speak for itself.

www.AwkwardMomentsBible.com/EndlessLoop

Across
5. Onan killed for his... (2)
10. Bloody Biblical beasts
11. Original flood epic
13. Missing 12 to 30
15. John's favorite food
16. Absent from the Garden
17. Upheld by Jesus
19. Object of wager
22. Angers Jesus
23. Righteous rape victims
24. Jesus' doppelganger
26. Best tasting bacon
27. We're instructed to hate...
29. King's ransom (3)
30. Arboreal victim (2)

Down
1. God performs for Moses (2)
2. Missing from tombs
3. Mothers during famine
4. If it offends you... (3)
6. Revered prophet of Qur'an
7. Lost, added, or rejected
8. Real food and drink
9. Mix & match scripture
12. Not much worker's comp
13. What saves Moses? (3)
14. Coitus + stripes? (2)
16. The perfect woman
18. Illogical logic
20. Victim's Dad says... (3)
21. Bald men's body guards
25. Failed prophecy
28. What women are made of

SOLUTION: http://www.AwkwardMomentsBible.com/V1crossword

Awkward Bible-Lib

INSTRUCTIONS: Using the clues provided, have one person ask other people for words to fill-in each blank - tweaking grammar as needed . Be sure *not* to read any of the story aloud or let anybody see the clues until *after* you have filled in all the blanks! **Then - read it out loud!**

There was a young man from ____city____ who was travelling with his ___woman's occupation___ .
They were __verb__ing in the town square when an old man __verb__ed them
and invited them to __verb__ at his house for the night.

They accepted the man's invitation and followed him home where they __verb__ed
their __animal__(s) before going inside to __verb__ their __body part__(s).

While they were __verb__ing, a crowd of men from the town began to __verb__ around the house,
yelling, "Bring out the man who is __verb__ing with you so we can __verb__ him."

The old man told them, "No, don't do such a/an __adjective__ thing! This man is a guest at my house!
Here, take my __adjective__ daughter and this man's __woman's occupation (re-use)__ .
You can __verb__ them and do whatever you like!"

But they wouldn't listen to the old man. The guest pushed his __woman's occupation (re-use)__
out the door and the town's men __verb__ed her all night long. They took turns __verb__ing
her until morning when she __verb__ed at the door of the house.

When the young man opened the door to leave, he found his __woman's occupation (re-use)__ ,
so he said, "Get up! It's time to go!" But she didn't __verb__ . So he put her on a/an __animal__
and took her back to __destination__ .

He used a/an __tool__ to __action__ his __woman's occupation (re-use)__'s body into __number__ pieces
and sent one piece to each __type of group/organization__ throughout __country or region__ .

YOU THINK YOUR STORY IS WEIRD? Read the real Bible verses and share your own online:
http://www.AwkwardMomentsBible.com/V1BibleLib

HORUS GILGAMESH was raised Catholic before being "born again" in college when he began following a calling toward full-time ministry. Early on, his efforts were focused on youth evangelism and Biblical literacy around the world. When he was on a missions trip to Africa, a fearless young boy approached, pleading, "Chakula? Maji?"- the Swahili words for "food" and "water." Unfortunately, Horus had no food or water to offer the poor child - only Bibles.

A few days later, Horus met a humanitarian relief worker from Spain who shared five simple words of wisdom that would change his life forever - *"Empty stomachs have no ears."* Horus realized that he was not meeting the very real needs of the people he was hoping to help - he was struggling to finding a purpose in his own life, as a self righteous servant of his Creator.

To many Christians, the most important gift you could ever give to a man is a chance at eternal life through the Gospel of Jesus Christ - the Living Water. But what about this life? There are billions who would give anything for a drink of regular old H2O.

Over the years, Horus became more interested in critical needs and social justice initiatives, helping those at risk of severe poverty, disease, or violence. The pain and suffering he saw first hand led him to be more and more troubled by God's apparent disregard for the children of His creation. This led Horus to years of re-studying the Bible for himself, away from the "rose-colored" teachings of any church or seminary. He never returned. *http://www.AwkwardMomentsBible.com/Horus*

AGNES TICKHEATHEN was mrpft ninln ul mbulsl aw pftul. (Sorry - it is difficult to understand her through the mask and ball gag. Check her out online!)
http://www.AwkwardMomentsBible.com/Agnes

Want More?

Cutting up concubines

Nephillim walking the earth

A head on a platter

Giving to the poor

Plagues, plagues, plagues

Baptism, bloody baptism

Suicide missions

Wives: What can you do?

Biblical Beastiality

Child abandonment

Monotheism made to order

Hearing God's voice(s)

Jonah and the ~~whale~~ fish

S██ - it's what's for dinner

Jesus: The Baby Killer

and many more...

AMCB - Volume #2

http://www.AwkwardMomentsBible.com/Vol2

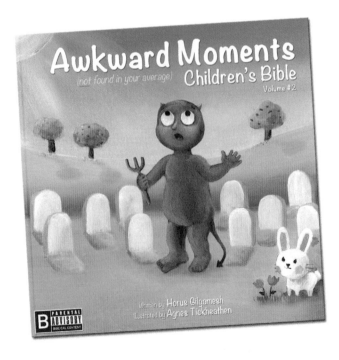

Awkward Moments
(not found in your average) Children's Bible
Volume #2

Written by Horus Gilgamesh
Illustrated by Agnes Tickheathen

PARENTAL ADVISORY
BIBLICAL CONTENT

33547732R00046

Made in the USA
Lexington, KY
28 June 2014